Tree-House Comix Proudly Presents

CAT KID COMIC CLUB

PERSPECTIVES

WRITTEN, ILLUSTRATED, AND COLORED BY

DAV PILKEY

AS GEORGE BEARD AND HAROLD HUTCHINS

WITH DIGITAL COLOR BY JOSE GARIBALDI

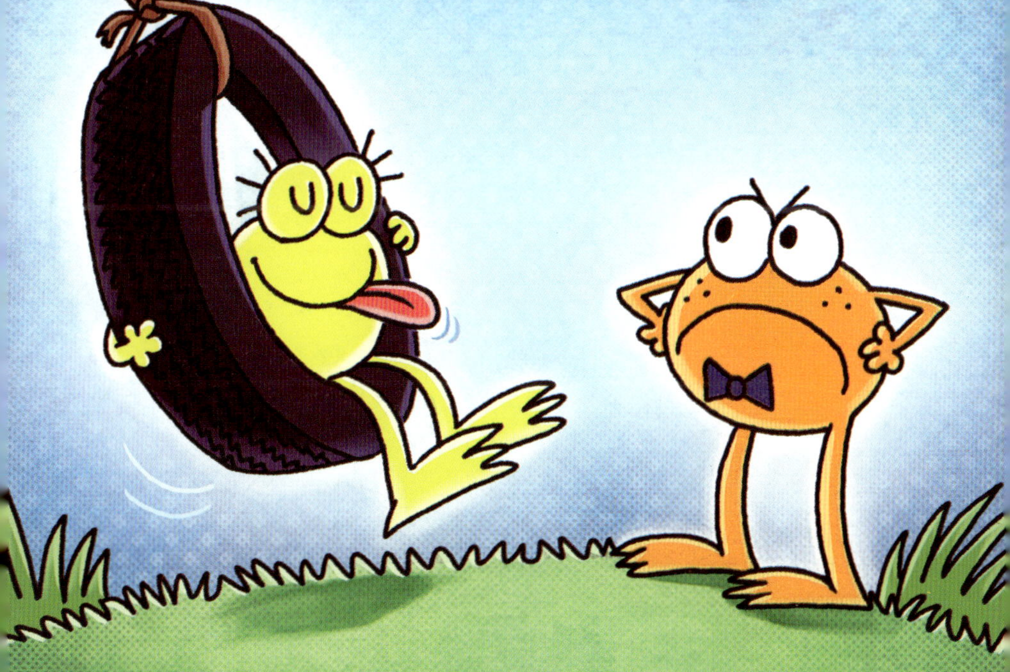

graphix

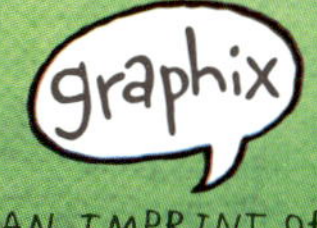

AN IMPRINT OF

SCHOLASTIC

Library of Congress Control Number 2021932630

ISBN: 978-93-5471-110-7

First edition, December 2021

This reprint edition: March 2026

Printed in India.

Illustrations and hand lettering by Dav Pilkey

Clay and paper models, Japanese calligraphy, photography, poetry, and paper cutouts by Dav Pilkey

All mini comics (except BABY FLIPPY) colored by Dav Pilkey using acrylic paints, colored pencils, ballpoint pens, markers, crayons, gouache, and watercolors.

Digital Color by Jose Garibaldi | Flatting by Aaron Polk
Special Thanks to: Arcana Izu and Asaba Ryokan

Editor: Ken Geist | Editorial Team: Megan Peace and Jonah Newman
Book design by Dav Pilkey and Phil Falco
Creative Director: Phil Falco
Publisher: David Saylor

Chapters & Comics

To my Mother, Barbara Pilkey,
and my Okaa-san, Yayoi Chiba

With two perspectives...
Warming sun and cooling rain
Many flowers bloom

–D.P.

CHAPTER 1

TIME WASTERS

What's up, Guys?

Welcome back to the SECOND week of...

...The CAT KID COMIC CLUB!

HOORAY!!!

I Know You all worked hard last weekend!

Does anybody have something they'd like to share?
OH! OH! OH!
OH! OH!

OKay, Melvin.

Naomi's KickinG me!

I AM NOT!
And now she's LYinG!

Naomi, would you please keep your feet to yourself?

Wow.

REALLY, Daddy?

You just...

...You just AUTOMATICALLY took HIS side.

You didn't even **ASK ME** if it was true.

It's --- it's...

...it's like I don't even matter.

I'm so sorry.

That was **VERY** wrong of me.

I should have asked you if it was true.

I Apologize!!!
I forgive You!!!

You didn't kick Melvin, did You?

Oh, yeah. I kicked him!

A whole buncha times!

NAOMi, KEEP YOUR FeeT to YOURSELF!

DADDY!!!

What is it NOW?

She called me a TATTLETALE!

Look— I'm TIRED of you Two FIGHTING all the time!!!

She started it.

IF YOU TWO DON'T STRAIGHTEN UP AND FLY RIGHT...

...You'll both spend the rest of the class...

...sitting on the time-out rock!!!

We're sorry, Daddy!

We won't fight anymore.

We'll be loving and kind from now on.

See?

Gee, Thanks for wasting all of that TIME, you GUYS!

We had a Whole Day of activities planned...
We did?

...but now we can't do it all...

...because of you TIME WASTERS!

Hey! "TIME WASTERS" is a really good idea for a comic!!!

I Guess the only thing we have time for now...

R-RiP
MOLLY

It looks pretty cool to me!
MOLLY

...but if you guys think it's **Boring**...

No! No! We want to learn how to write our names like that!
Yeah!

Say you're sorry, Drake!
Sorry!

Alright, then!

First, we need a volunteer.
Me! Me! Pick me!
PLEEEASE! Me!
Me! Me! Me!
Pick me!
OH!
OH! OH!
OH!

Umm, I choose Pink!
Yessss!

Okay, now write your name.
R-RIP

My full name?
No. Just "Pink."

Pink

Now use this marker to draw a line...
PINK

...AROUND each letter.

Hey! I'm making Bubble Letters!
PINK

Now, erase the Pencil letters You drew first!
RUB RUB
RUB

COOOOL!
PINK

But how do I make it look 3-D?
That's the fun part!

Now draw lines from the edges of your letters...

PINK
This is EASY!!!

Hey! I wanna try!!!
Me too!!!

And so...

Hey! I did it!
WENDY
Sweet!

I colored in the 3-D Part!
EL
COOL!

I Gave my balloon letters blocky edGes!
KiP
How'd Ya do that?
KiP
Skill!
I just figured out a trick!
What?
If You don't want Your letters to Go to infinity...
RAiNE
... Just draw a line across...
RAiNE
... and erase the triangle part!
RAiNE
Nice!
Rub
Rub Rub

NAOMI the GREAT
MELVIN RULES

NAOMI the GREAT
MELVIN RULES

Hey, I need your eraser.
NAOMI the GREAT
MELVIN RULES

Rub
Rub
Rub
MELVIN RULES

Rub
Rub
Rub
MELVIN RULES

Don't use it ALL UP!!!
Rub Rub
Rub
MELVIN RULES

FOOooo

DADDY!

What is it Now, Melvin?
SHE USED UP MY WHOLE ERASER...
...Then She blew eraser Stuff ALL OVER Me!
IT WAS AN ACCIDENT!
NO, IT WASN'T!
ALRIGHT, THAT DOES IT!!!

I've HAD it UP TO HERE with YOU TWO!

RAine?

Yes, Daddy?

Would You please come down here...

... and Switch seats with Melvin?

WHY DO *I* HAVE TO SWITCH SEATS?

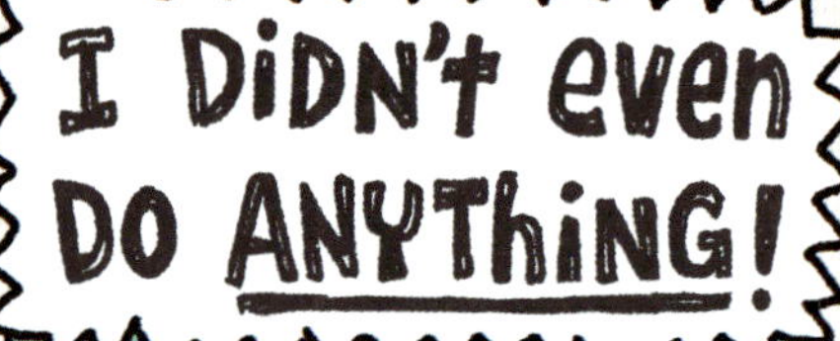
I DIDN'T even DO ANYTHING!

Melvin, Don't argue with me!!!

NO FAIR!

HA! HA! Melvin Got in trou-bLe!!!

And, NAOMi?

You can Go Sit on the Time-Out Rock!

Why? What DiD I DO?

Oh, wait. I Remember now.

OK, See Ya!!!

TiME OUT.

WE'RE GONNA START OVER TOMORROW...

CHAPTER 2

MORE GOOFING AROUND

The next day...

HEY!

You kids PROMISED to behave yourselves TODAY!!!

We know.

But we didn't really mean it.
Yeah. We just say stuff sometimes.

... and You can all spend the rest of the day...

Wow.
Their enthusiasm warms my heart.

OKAY, GUYS, TODAY IS A DO-OVER!

But before we begin...

...Does Anybody have A COMIC they'd like to share?

We Do! We Do!
TIME WASTERS:
Wasters of time

We made a Comic last NiGht!!!

Time wasters:
wasters of time
By Curly and Gilbert

One time at School...
Felix and Jax...
...I want You to write a Report...
...on the Great Chicago fire of 1871.
aw, maaan!
What a RiP!
I wish we didn't have to write that report.
me too!

Hey! I know! Let's build a time machine.
OK
We can go back in time and Prevent that fire...
...then we won't have to write about it.
Sweeeet!
and so...
Bang Bang
Time machine
screw screw
ALL done!!
Hooray!
Time machine
Time Machine
Let's Go
OK

My Phone says the fire started on October 8, 1871 at 8:30 pm.
Let's set the controller for 2 hours Before the fire started!
CLICK CLICK CLICK
6:30 pm Chicago
If we use our time wisely...
... we can save hundreds of Lives...
137 Dekove Stree
click click
...And we won't have to Learn anything!!!
Nice!
and so...
Time machine
ZAP

Soon...
Welcome to Chicago
Time machine
Here we are, back in old-timey Chicago!
It sure is Boring here!
I know
Hey! Let's play a Game on my Phone!
OK
Pew Pew Pew
Pew Pew Pew
Pew Pew
my turn!
Pew Pew Pew
Pew Pew
Pew

6:44 pm
Pew Pew
Pew Pew
Pew
7:19 pm
Pew Pew
Pew Pew
Pew Pew
8:26 pm
Pew Pew
Pew Pew
Pew Pew
WE DID it!!!
We saved the
GALAXY!!!!
HEY! How come
it's not updating?
THERE'S NO
Wi-Fi!!!

Quick! Let's Go Back Before we Lose our Progress!
HURRY!
Time machine
Time machine
ZAP
POOF!
SSSSS
FOOSH
crackle crackle
ROAR

Soon...
Time machine
We're BACK!
The Next Morning
SCHOOL
Here's our Report, teacher!
Report
THE Great CHICAGO Fire
by Jax and Felix
It was very, very very, very, very, very, very, very, very, very, very very Boring. PLUS, No Wi-Fi. Booo! The End.
aw, Maaan!
F
TIME WASTERS

That was... uh...
INTERESTING!

AND
EDUCATIONAL!

Boys, that WAS
NOT Educational!
Yes it was!

I'll PROVE it!
Hey, Pedro...

...Where did the
Great Chicago
Fire take place?

Ummm...

Chicago?

I rest my case!
SLAP!

OKAY—Anybody else???

We finished OUR comic, too!

We've been working on it for almost A WHOLE WEEK!

And it's called...

CHUBBS McSPIDERBUTT
WRITTEN AND DIRECTED BY The HACKER BROS.

Then one day he accidentally sat on a SPIDER named Jake.

AW, GREAT!

Now Your Spidery venom...

...is transforming my butt!!!

It's Getting SPIDER-iER...

... AND SPIDER-iER!

THANKS A LOT, JAKE!
Gee Whiz! I Said I was Sowwy!!!

Well **NOW** what am I supposed to do?

You could be a superhero!!!

Hey! That's a Good idea!!!

Thanks, Jake!
No Prob!

So Jake and Chubbs bought an old van...

...and customized it!
CHUBBS & JAKE

This Van has it **ALL !!!!!**
CHUBBS & JAKE

Smiley-faced Grill?
Check!

Froyo-Smoothie Station?
Check!
CHUBBS & JAKE

CHUBBS & JAKE
Indoor Disco Dance Studio?
Check!

But Wait! ...

What's this?

SSSSSSHHH!

Who the heck is THAT?

It is I, Doctor Pasty McSprinkles...

...Supreme Leader of the N.V.N.C.

What's the N.V.N.C?

N.V.N.C
The Not Very Nice Club!!!

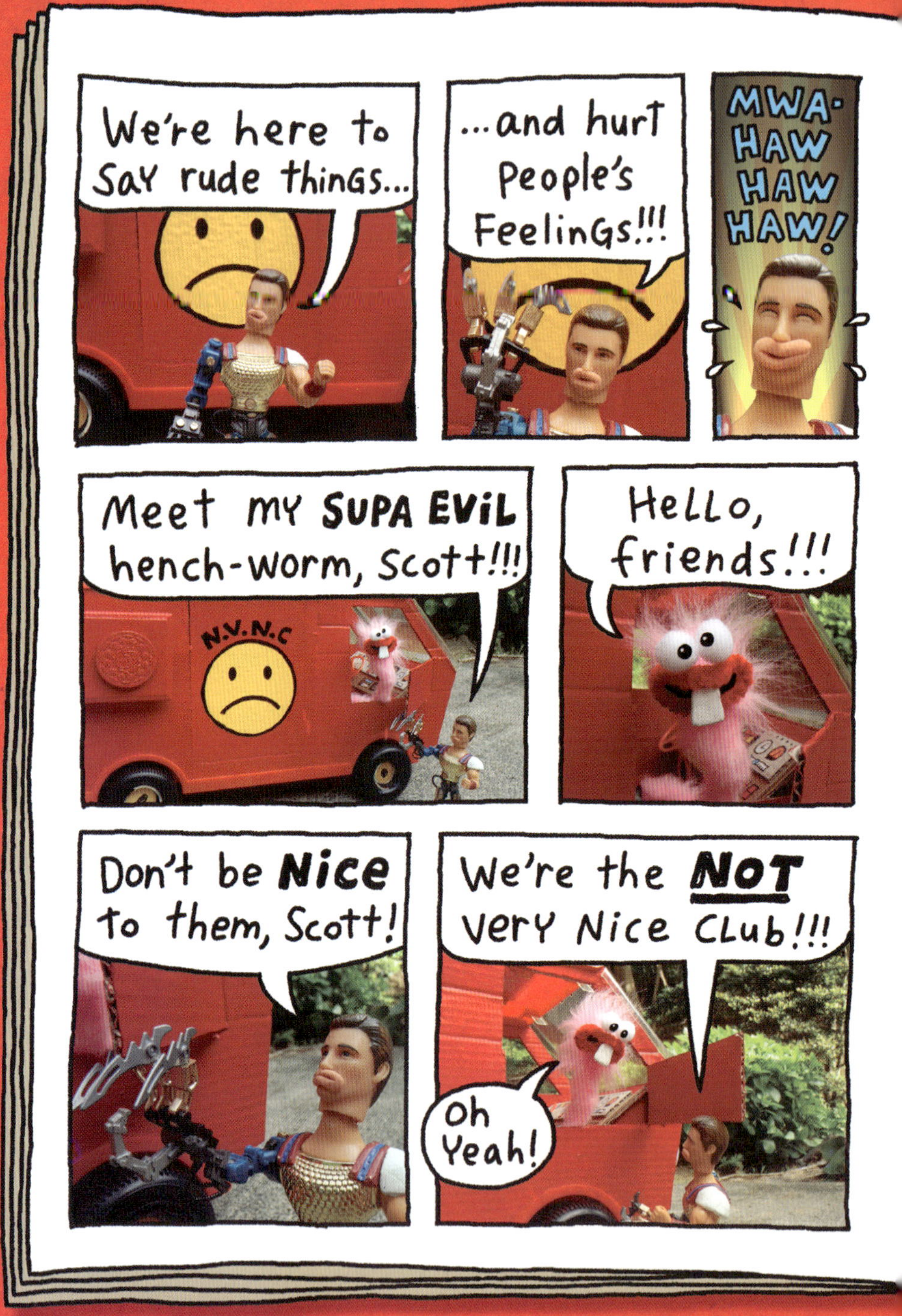

We're here to SAY rude thinGS...

And now we shall proceed with our MERCILESS TAUNTING!
HAW HAW!

You GUYS look WEIRD!

I'll bet YA SMELL weird, too!!!!!!!

Yeah! Like FRESH STRAWBERRIES!

SCOTT! STOP SAYING Nice THINGS, OKAY?
Oops. Oh, Yeah!

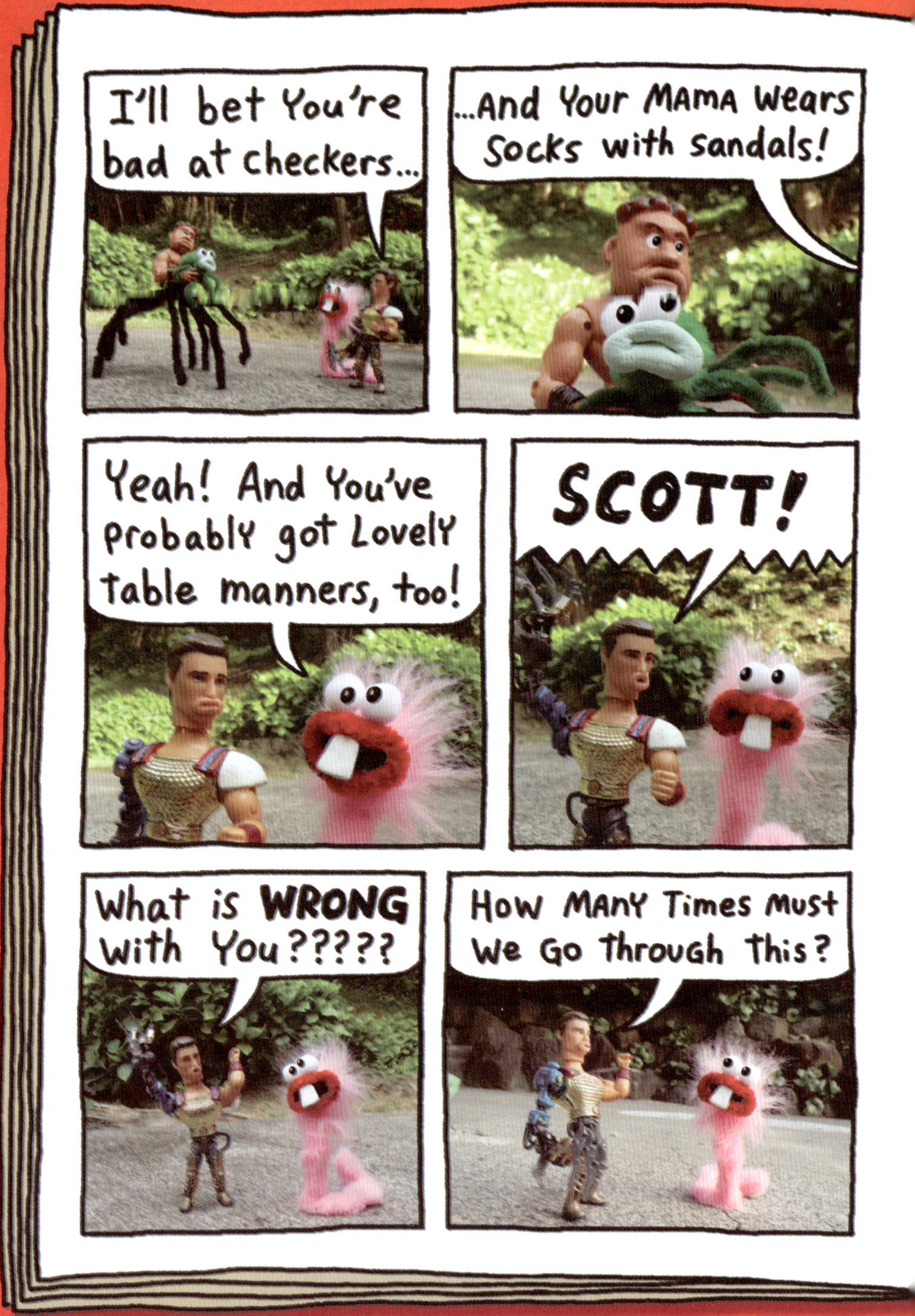

Yeah! And You've probably got Lovely table manners, too!

If You want to be in this club...

...then You need to FOCUS!
I'll try.

Your breath is stinky.

That's PERFECT! —but say it to THEM, Not ME!

His breath is Stinky!
SCOTT!

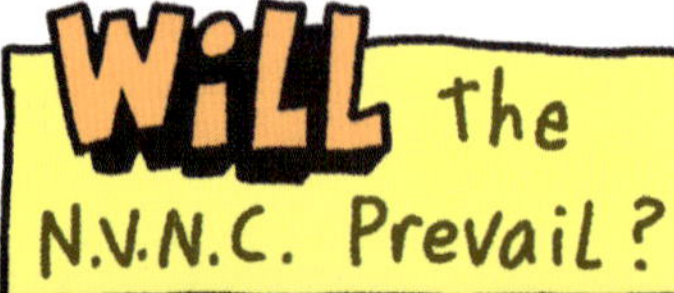

Will the N.V.N.C. Prevail?

Will our heroes Get their feelings hurt?

Will Scott ever Learn to be Rude?

Find out Soon in our NEXT chapter:
CHUBBS & JAKE

ChuBBS McSPiDerButt 2
The Birth of Big Bubba Babyhead

Hey, You GUYS should work with ME!

We don't wanna work with You, Naomi!!!

Yeah!

'Cuz you always try to be the BOSS of Everybody!
Besides, we're the HACKER BROTHERS!

GENDER DISCRIMINATION!

WHAT'S GOING ON NOW?

They won't let me work with them 'cuz I'm a GIRL!

Who WON'T?
Gilbert and Rico and Drake!!!

We'll see about THAT!

Who's the tattle-tale NOW?

WHAT'S the Problem, BOYS?

Daddy, it's NOT Because she's a GIRL!!!

We don't wanna work with ANY-BODY ELSE!

Yeah! We're not discriminating against Her...

...We discriminate against EVERYbody!

You shouldn't say it like that!
Oh.

Naomi, I can't Force them to work with You.

OKAY, FiNE!

I'LL MAKE MY OWN COMiC!

...AND it'LL be WAY Better than YOURS!

I'm very Proud of Y—

HEY!

Why are YOU still sitting here?
This is my seat!

I told you to sit up there, yesterday!
But- But- But-

NO BUTS!!! Get back up there NOW!

Aw, PLEASE let me stay here, Daddy!

Pleeeeeease?

I Promise I'll be GOOD!

I Promise I won't FiGHT!

I Promise I won't TATTLe!

PLease PLease
se PLease PLea
PLease PLease

... OKaY.

Wow! You made a lot of Promises...

...but I didn't!!!

CHAPTER 3

New Day, New Perspective

OKay, GuYs! Today is a new day...

...and This Time, We're Gonna be SERiOUS!!!

So NO FiGhTinG... NO TATTLinG...
...And NO TiMe WASTiNG!
aw, maaan!

So-does anybody have a new comic to share?

We Do!

SUPA FAIL 2
OLD LAdy's Revenge
F
BY K.T.,
Kip & CurLY

GOOD Afternoon.
President
F

AS most of You remember...

...The world blew up yesterday.
President
F

it did?
I forgot all about that.

BUT Today, every-thing is back to normal...

...thanks to Supa Fail!!!
President
F

How'd You save the world, Supa Fail?
Well, I'll tell You.
I was Floating around in space...
...When I remembered I had Tape in my Pocket.
So I grabbed a chunk of earth...
... and taped it to another earth Chunk.

I Kept taping one chunk...
...to another...
Japan
cleveland
AusTralia
...until everything was back to normal.
North Pole
OHio
EQUATOR
...sort of.
Earth
You're our Hero, Supa Fail!!!
Oh, Yeah?
OLd Lady's House

I can't stand him...

He Foiled MY RoBBery Plan!
News
ToothPick saved!

But I will Get my Revenge!!!
Haw
Haw
Haw

So she went down to her secret Laboratory...

...And created a evil invention.
clank
clank
clank

I call it: the Polluter computer!

Go, my precious, evil computer...

...Go and Pollute the Earth!!!
O.K.

And so...
HeLP!
SMOG

Toxic waste
aw maaan!

Green House GAS
This looks like a Job for...
SUPA FAIL!
Here I Am!
BOING
I'LL Stop the Polluter computer!!!

Oh Yeah???
I Shall STOMP YOU OUT!!!
...With MY CARBON FOOTPRINT!

STOMP

YAAAAA!

STAMP

Everything Seemed Hopeless!!!!!
but then...

Supa FAiL found something in his Pocket!

CARbon TACKS

Toss
Carbon Tacks

WHAM!
F
OWie
OWie OWie OWie
BoinG BoinG
BoinG
BoinG
DanGer: CLiFF
F

YAAAAAAAAA
CRASH
I win!!!
Not so Fast, Supa Fail!
OLd LadY!
Look Down!!!

Danger: CLiff
HAW HAW HAW HAW
HAW HAW HAW HAW!
SSSSSSSSSSSSSSSSSSS
Tina's Nuclear Power Plant
Run!
It's Gonna BLOW!
Don't Miss our Next thrilling chapter:
SUPA FAiL 3
GOODBYE CRUEL WORLD
coming soon!!!

HOORAY!!!

That was AWESOME!
Aw, maaaan!!!

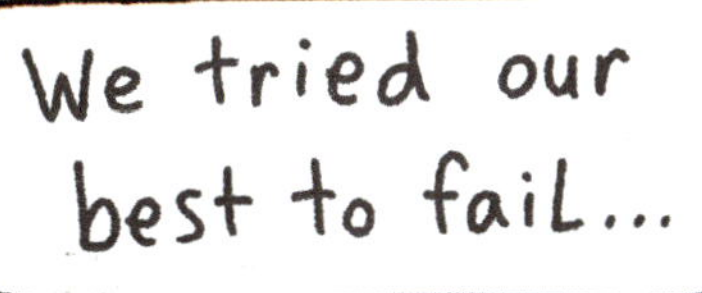
We tried our best to fail...

...but I guess we didn't succeed!!!

You just blew my mind, dude.

Well, I think it's GREAT that You Kids are IMPROVING!

Even Your DRAWINGS Are Getting better!

Look at the PERSPECTIVE on this building!

Curly drew that, not me.

Hey, Curly, Can You show us how to draw like that?

OKAY!

First, You draw the Ground...

...then, You make a building, which is just a rectangle.

Then, add some square windows.

Now, put a dot on the Ground...

...and draw a line from the edge...

...to the dot.

Quit touching me!

Oh. So You DON'T want me to touch You?
NO!

OKay!

WHAT ARe YOU DOiNG ???

I'm NOT Touching You.

...Now draw a line at the back of the building...

...then erase the leftover part.
Rub
Rub
Rub

I'm still not touching you!

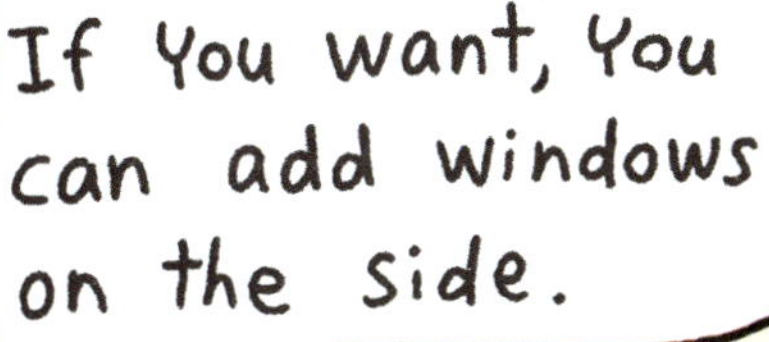
If you want, you can add windows on the side.

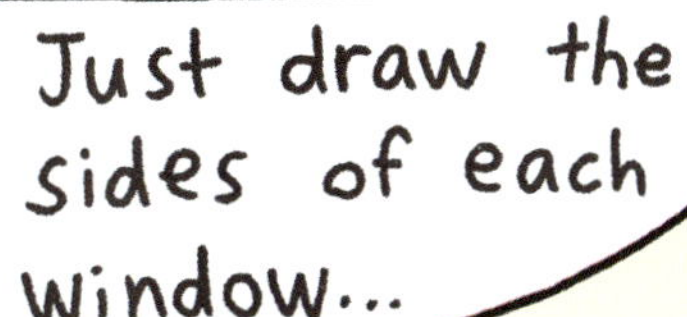
Just draw the sides of each window...

... and connect the tops and bottoms of each side...

... to the dot.

Now, draw the other side of each window...

... then erase all of the extra lines.
Rub
Rub
Rub

Can we use Rulers?

Yeah, if You want to.

Still Not touching You...

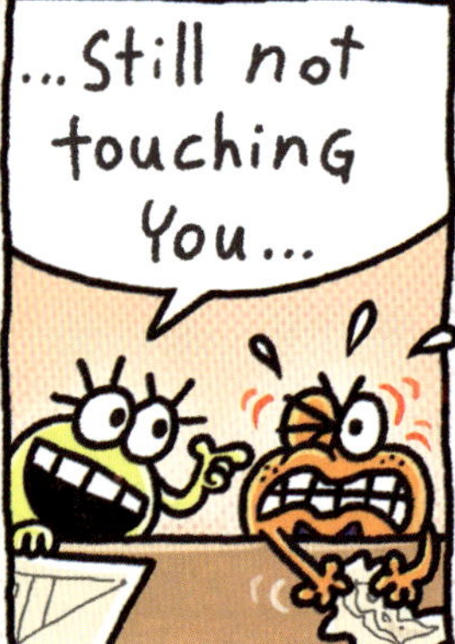
...Still not touching You...

... Still not touching—
CRUMPLE
CRUMPLE

YOU'RE DRIVING ME CRAZY!!!

CHAPTER 4

Big Trouble for Little Melvin

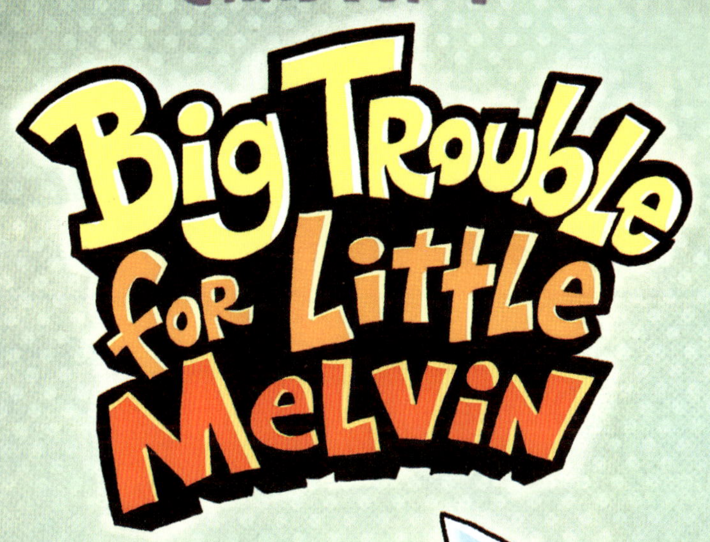

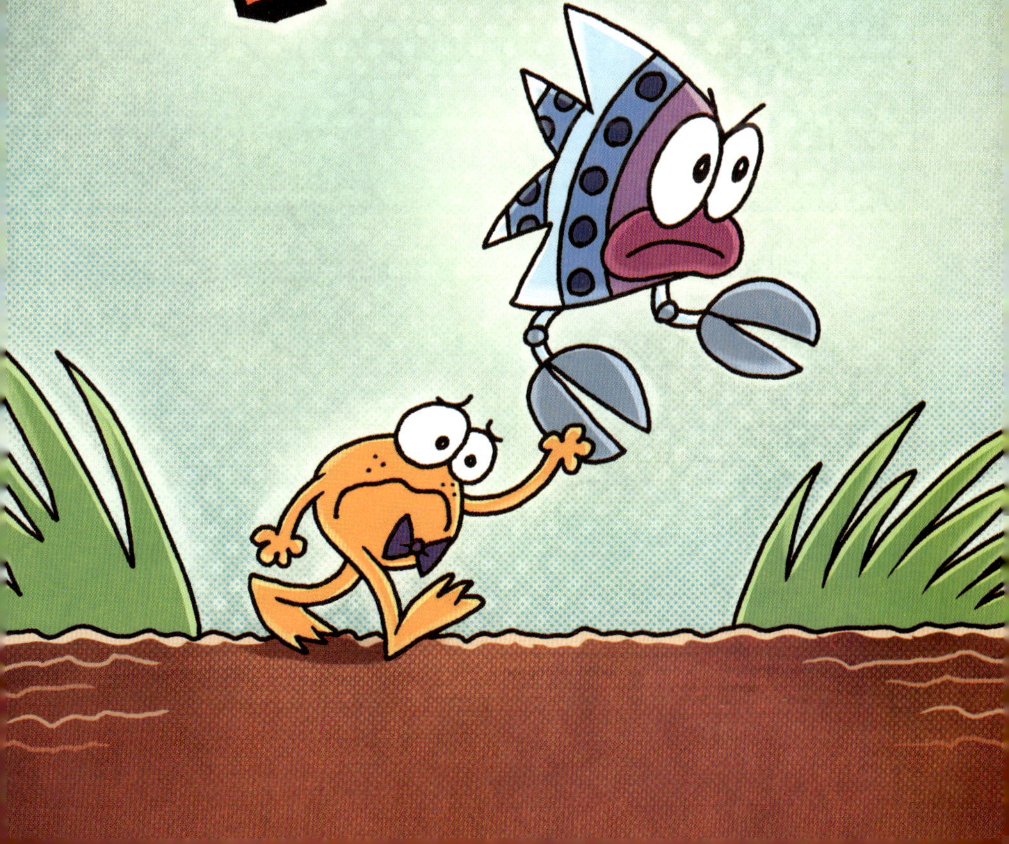

WHAT IS GOING ON???

She's not touching me!

He **TOLD** me not to touch him...

... So I didn't!

I was just trying to respect his wishes!
SHE WAS NOT!!!

Melvin, come with me.

WHY? WHAT FOR?

We need to have a little talk, buddy.

And so...

WAIT--- Where are we GOING?
TIME OUT.

Melvin, You need to sit here and think about—
TIME OUT.

DADDY---NO! PLEASE!!!

Melvin, DON'T ARGUE With-

But, DADDY- I've NeveR had to Sit there before!

You hAven't?

NeveR! Not even ONCe!!!

I'm the only kid in our family with a **PERFECT RECORD!**

It WASn't even MY FAULT!!!

SHE StARted it!

All I Wanted to do was Draw with PersPective!!!

Melvin, PERSPECTIVE isn't just About DRAWING!!!

It's also about UNDERSTANDING!

It's about seeing the world from Someone ELSE'S Point of view!!!
Time out.

Hey!

Would You still like to do a Different Punishment?
Time out.
Yes! Yes! Yes! Yes! Ye

OKay. Then You can make a comic...

...About Naomi...

...from HER PERSPECTIVE!

AND it Better NOT BE MEAN!

I don't WANNA DO THAT!!!

Then take a seat, buddy!
Time Out.

AL-RIGHT!! I'LL MAKE THE COMIC!!!

And it's due by FRIDAY!!!

This just Gets worse And Worse!

CHAPTER 5

Hurry up, bug breath!
MY Sister, Naomi

We're Gonna be late for Comic Club!!!

HOLD STill, I SAID!

MY Sister, Naomi

Are You Almost done?
Yeah. With the cover!

Let me see it!

HEY!

Why'd You MAKE MY MOUTH SO BiG?
MY sister, Naomi
by Melvin The Frog

Your mouth IS biG!

Let me see the inside!

Naomi is

THAT'S ALL YOU WROTE SO FAR?

I couldn't think of anything that wasn't mean.

How am I EVER Gonna finish this?

I Know! Write about how much You love me!

I Don't Love You!
You don't?

NO! You're the most Annoying Frog in the WHOLE WORLD!

So if some big monster came out of those woods...

...and wanted to beat me up...

...You wouldn't try to protect me?

OF COURSE I WOULD!

NoBody Messes with MY Sister!

That means You love me!!!

Hey, wait up!!!
My sister, Naomi

This thing is due Tomorrow!!!

How am I supposed to finish it???
My sister, Naomi
by Melvin the Frog

Beats me!

It should be easy for You since Ya love me so much!
My sister, Naomi

CHAPTER 6

Sister Stories

And so...
Hey! You kids are **LATE!**

It was his fault!
WAS NOT!!!

Well, you missed the first part of Poppy's new comic!

It's okay, Molly!
Skelepup
By Poppy

I'll start over!

Skelopup
BY POPPY

One time there was a reaLLY, reaLLy old Dog...

...Who died.
KLUNK

And everybody was sad and stuff.
OLD DOG

But they didn't need to be...
OLD DOG

...because they didn't know...

...That the really, really old dog's story...
...was just getting started.
OLD DOG

Soon, the Dog met a cloud.
Hi!
It's time to go.
what's your name?
But the DOG could not remember.
That's okay. I'll call you Skelopup!
Yawn

While they Flew…

…Skelopup got sleepier…

… and sleepier.

Soon he was dreaming of his old Life.

He dreamed about Fun stuff…

… and happy stuff…

… and sad stuff.

But then it all faded away.
when Skelopup woke up...
They were in Deadville.
It had a swing set...
... and a fun water slide...

... and Yummy Tacos.
munch munch
Taco Death
munch munch
See Ya Later, skelopup!!!
Skelopup played and played.
It was Fun.
But sometimes...
...skelopup felt kind of Sad.

Then one day...
Skelopup met a Little Ghost Girl.
I'm so sad...
...because my really, really old cat...
old cat
... isn't dead anymore.
old cat
So they were sad together.
old cat

But they didn't need to be.
old cat
Because They didn't Know...
...That the really, really old cat's story...
...was just Getting Started.
old cat
Lick
Lick
Lick
old cat

So Skelopup and the little Ghost Girl walked together...
... and ate together...
Taco Death
crunch munch crunch
... and played together.
And after a while...
...Things didn't feel so sad anymore.
The end.

HOW TO DRAW Skelopup

in 14 supa easy steps.

How to **DRAW**

The Little Ghost Girl in 14 Supa easy Steps

ABOUT The CREATOR:

Poppy

Poppy is a frog who likes to make up Ghost stories. She also likes pizza but with **NO** cheese because she is Lactose intolerant and it makes ~~me~~ her throw up.

Wow, Poppy! That was AWESOME!
Thanks!

Any other thoughts?

I liked the "TACO Death" Restaurant!
Me too!

I was hungry when I wrote that part!!!
Skelopup
By Poppy

Is that what REALLY happens when you die?

Beats me! I was just using my imagination.
Oh.

OKAY, who's next?

I made a comic with WendY!!!

It's all about DaddY's AmazinG Adventures...
...When he was just a little baby!

I drew the pictures...
... and I adapted the story!

Baby
Flippy
A True Story by
Wendy & Raine

One time there was a baby fish named Flippy.
He was the smallest fish in his neighborhood.
And sometimes...
...the bigger fish were mean to him.
Hey Fish Face!
Look at the baby fish face!!!
What's up, fish face?

Boo-Hoo-Hoo!!!
HA! HA! HA! HA! HA!
Baby Flippy would swim home crying.
Fortunately, his mom always knew the right thing to say.
Remember, son...
It's not the size of your body that counts.
It's the size of your heart.

Baby Flippy tried his best not to be afraid.
But as he grew older...
...his bullies grew fiercer.
GET HIM!!!
Baby Flippy swam with all his strength.

Suddenly, he spied an old, clay pot.
Quickly, he zipped inside for safety...
WE'VE GOT YOU NOW!!!
But THEN...

Eight horrible arms emerged from the clay pot.
SWIM AWAY!!!
SWIM AWAY!!!
SWIM AWAY!!!
Baby Flippy was paralyzed with fear.
He wanted to swim away, too, but he couldn't move.

Then suddenly...
YANK
ZIP!
The clay pot was pulled to the surface...
...with Baby Flippy stuck inside!
SPLASH
HOORAY!!! WE CAUGHT A GIANT OCTOPUS!!!

A man put a heavy lid onto the clay pot...
...and the boat sped quickly away.
Baby Flippy looked through the tiny holes on the lid...
...and saw the sky growing darker...
...and darker.

Soon, lightning shattered the sky, and wild waves crashed around the boat.
Put that octopus below deck!
Aye, aye, Captain!
The man picked up the heavy clay pot.
And Baby Flippy saw his chance.
Quickly, he swam up...

...and leaped through a tiny hole in the lid.
FLIP!
PLOP!
AAAAH!
EEEEE!
OOOOOH!!!
THERE'S A FISH IN MY SHIRT!
CRASH

I've Got You Now!
THWAK
NO! NO!
KA BOOM
YAAAAAAAAAA!

ZAP!
...To be continued.

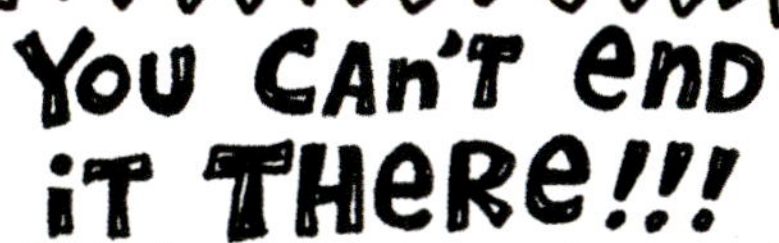

YEAH! It WAS JUST GeTTinG to The GOOD PART!

But we'll continue it next week!

NEXT Week?

We HAVE to WAIT A WHOLE Week?

ALRiGHT, ALRiGhT!

Settle down, YA Weirdos!

Wendy and Raine just ended their comic DRAMATiCALLY!

That's called a CLiffhANGer!

It makes readers excited to Return to the next episode!

It Just made Me MAD!!!
Yeah! Me too!!!

Did all of that stuff REALLY happen, Daddy?

Well, MOST of it did.

Except for the LIGHTNING and the SHARK!

We just wanted to spice things up a little.

OKAY. But you can't call it a TRUE STORY...

...if you make up a bunch of stuff.
Oh.

Can we say "BASED" on a True story?

I Guess that would be okay.

Sweeeet!!!

Things Are Gonna Get SPiCY!!!

Does AnYbody else have a Comic to share?

We made a new HAiKU-PHOTO COMiC!

SHODO GARDENS
PHOTOS POEMS AND CALLIGRAPHY BY SUMMER AND STARLA

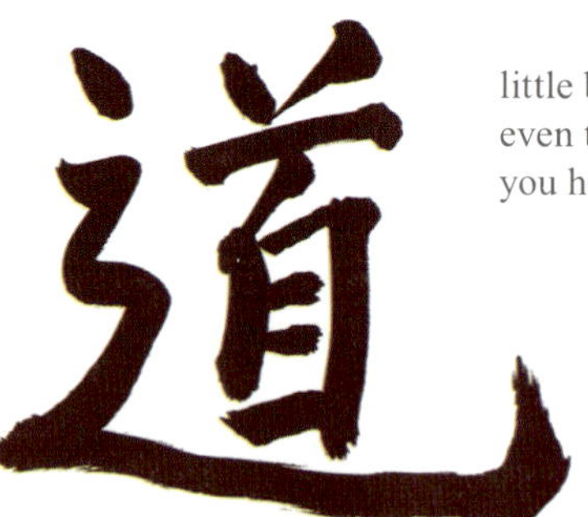

little blade of grass
even though the world is hard
you have found a way

努力

one good photograph
comes to those who dare to take
a thousand bad ones

bold, black butterfly
spread your wings in the morning
and bathe in the sun

自信

if you're the pink one
don't worry about the rest.
just be the pink one

花火

garden fireworks
bursting bright in clouds of moss
nature celebrates

Haiku and Shodo
are types of Japanese art
with structure and rules.

but with these two arts,
feeling is more important
than anything else.

one must know the rules
in order to move past them.
learn, then step beyond...

Each Shodo character can have many meanings.
These are some meanings for the ones we painted:

道 Way, means, road

努力 Try hard + Power = Endeavor

開 Open or unfold

自信 Self-confidence [+ Trust]

花火 Flower + Fire = Fireworks

Nao'omi Kuratani, Akemi Kobayashi, Shunsuke Okunishi, *A New Dictionary of Kanji Usage* (Tokyo: Gakken Co., LTD., 1982).

Summer and Starla would like to acknowledge and thank the artists who inspired them recently, including:

Shoko Kanazawa, who is one of Japan's most highly respected Shodo artists. She paints from her heart with giant brushes. She also has Down's syndrome.

And

Shozo Sato, author of *Shodo: The Quiet Art of Japanese Zen Calligraphy* (Rutland: Tuttle Publishing, 2014).

Wow! That was COOOOOL!!!
Thanks!

I liked those stick drawings!

They're not sticks. They're Japanese words.
Oh.

Will you show us how to write them?

No way! I'm too shy.

I'll do it!!!

We learned it from a library book!

First, you get your watercolors and a brush...

...add some water...

...then you gotta get your **MIND** ready!

Take deep breaths...

...Snifffff...

Huuuhhhhh...

...Get chiller...

...and chiller...

...Then, when you're totally chilled...

...begin.

Try to write with your feelings.
OH! OH!
How do you know what you're writing?
I memorized this one.
It means: "Sit First, Dash Seven."
Oh.

Chapter 7

The Inspiration

OKay, Good Job, everybody! We'll see you tomorrow!

Hey! Tomorrow's FRIDAY!!!

Are we Going to have another Show and Tell Party?

Daddy won't let us because we were goofing around too much this week.
AW, MAAAN!
NO FAIR!

It's mostly Melvin and Naomi's fault!!!
YeAh!

Thanks A LOT, You Guys!!!

We can't have a Party because of YOU TWO!!!
YeAH!

Gee whiz! I feeL SOOO TeRRibLe...

...I'm Gonna Go cry now.

HEY, wait up!

Where are You GoinG?
FLea Market.

WHY?
I need Some more inspirations for the comic I'm makinG.

You're supposed to be helping ME with MY COMIC!

Sorry, dude. You're on your own!!!
TODAY
FLEA MARKET
PRIZES
GAMES
FOOD
FUN

How am I supposed to write about you?

I don't even know anything about you!!!

50¢ each
75¢ each
TOYS
GAME OF SKILL
Not my problem.

HeY, SluGGER!

Do You want to win Some balloons for Your Girlfriend?

She's my sister!

Just Give it a shot, buddY!!!

I'll Give You a balloon for each can You Knock over!

OkaY!

WHOOSH!

Give it another try, sport!!!

SWOOOF

You did an AMAZING JOB!
I did?

You're a NATURAL!
PAT PAT PAT
I am?

You deserve a REWARD for TrYinG so Hard!
I do?

Here You Go, Son!
Thanks!

Would You like to TRY AGAIN?

Hey! It's MY TURN!!!

Let Me try!!!

HAW HAW HAW
HAW
HAW

WATCH out, everybody!

This Little Girly thinks she can—

ZOOO
And So...
Hey!
That Guy Said You could have this.

OOM
SWISH
Heyyyyy...

I wonder why I Got three balloons...

...but You only Got **ONE**.

That doesn't seem fair.

Gee, Ya think?

Here. Take one of mine.

Now it's fair.

WOW! Thanks, MELVIN!!!

YOU'RE MY HERO!

This Fixes EVERYTHING!

HEY!

What Did YA DO THAT FOR?

That GUY WAS A JERK!!!

I thought he was nice.

Yeah, to YOU!!!

All he did was PRAISE And ENCOURAGE you!!!

He Never even SPOKE to ME!
He didn't?

AND YOU DIDN'T EVEN NOTICE!

Welcome to MY WORLD, Melvin!

Girls have to work HARDER than boys...

...And we STILL Get Less!!!

Less Respect... Less MONEY...

...Less FREEDOM ...Less Opportunities...

... and dopes like you
NEVER EVEN NOTICE!!!

Is that why you hate me so much?

I don't hate you.

You're, like, the world's most funnest person to fight with!

I am?
Yeah!

Look, Melvin...

... I'm not just some little Girl who can't do AnYthinG about this!

I'm GoinG to make CHANGE in the world.

So I've Got to be readY...

...to
Fight.

Every.

Day.

Thanks to You, I Get Lots of Practice!

Hey!!!

I Know What I'm GONNA MAKE MY COMIC ABOUT!!

CHAPTER 8

The Saddest Friday of All Time

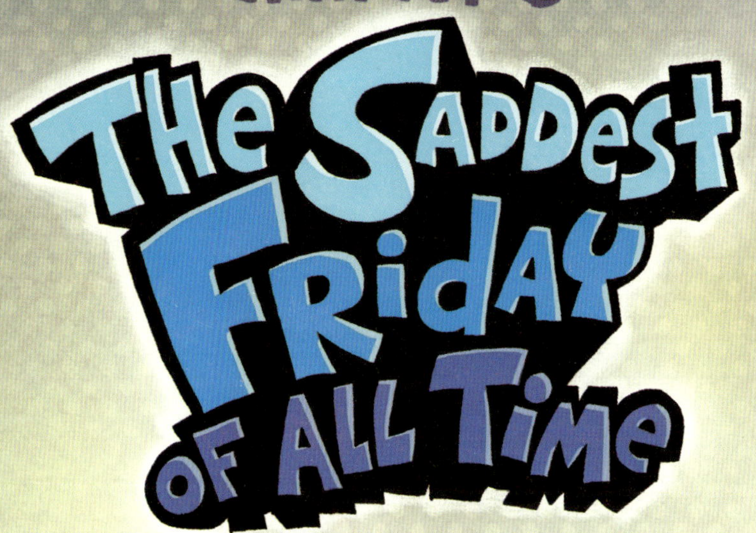

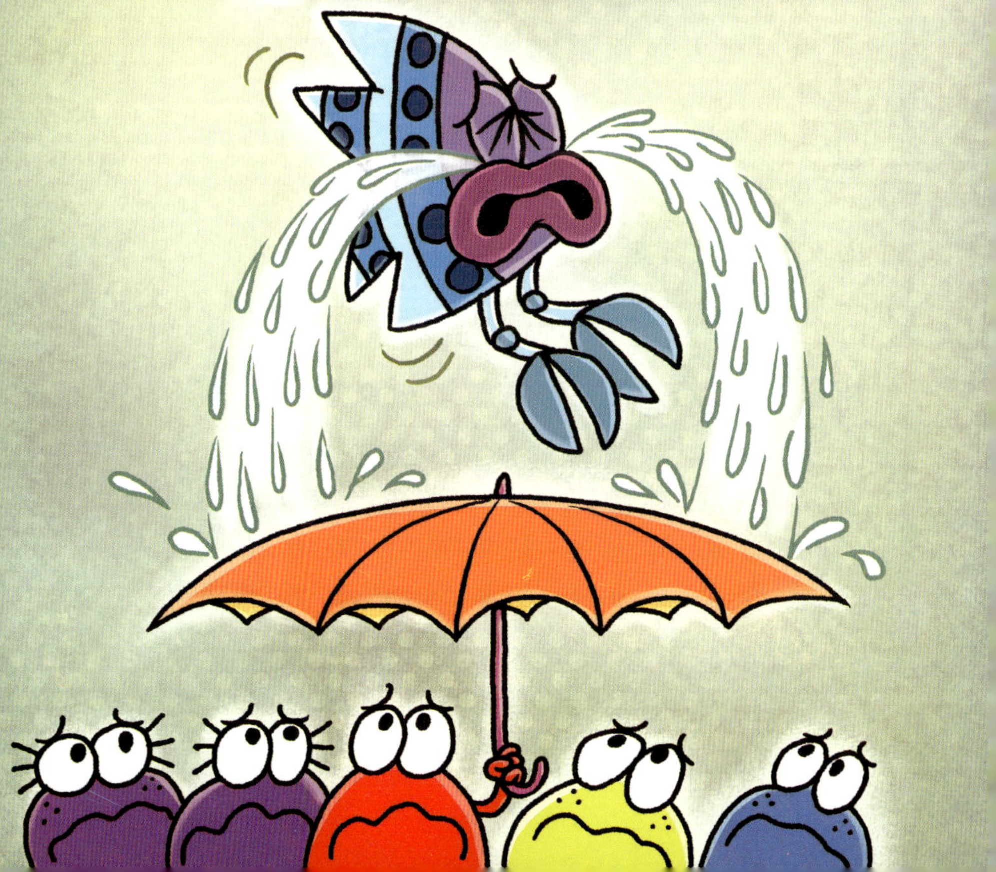

The next day...
Where the heck are Melvin and Naomi?

Yeah! They were supposed to be here TEN MINUTES AGO!

THIS is why we're NOT having a Party!

You Kids have been VERY NAUGHTY this week!!!

FIGHTING...
WASTING Time...

...GOOFING AROUND... BREAKING PROMISES... SHOWING UP LATE...

It's Mostly Melvin and Naomi's Fault!
Yeah!

No...

...it's ... it's...

... it's MY FAULT!!!

I've been trying to raise you kids...

...to be kind and responsible...

...but... but...

...I must be the world's **WORST** father!

BOO-HOO-HOO-HOO-HOO-HOO

Well that was depressing.

Hey! Let's all Cheer Daddy up!

Good idea!
Come on, Gang!
Let's Go!!!

We're sorry, Daddy.

I Know.

It's not **YOUR** fault that we're naughty!
I blame society!
Me too!

...and I was really sad?

Yes.

Well, maybe...

... Since you're feeling sad...

...We could read you some of OUR STORIES...

That would be very nice.

US FIRST!!!
US FIRST!!!

Squid Kid and Katydid

by MOLLY and LI'L Petey

One time two people wanted to have a baby.

Squid kid was happy at home...
S.K.

...but the neighbor-hood was another story.

You Look weird, SQUID KID!!!
Yeah! Get Lost Ya weirdo!!!

Boo Hoo Hoo Hoo!
HA HA HA HA HA!

Meanwhile, at Bug School...

...Katydid was also having trouble.

Everyone else sat still...

...but Katydid didn't.
Boing

Everyone else paid attention...

Everyone else Learned the same way...

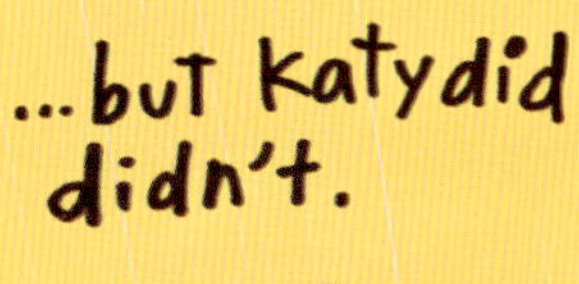

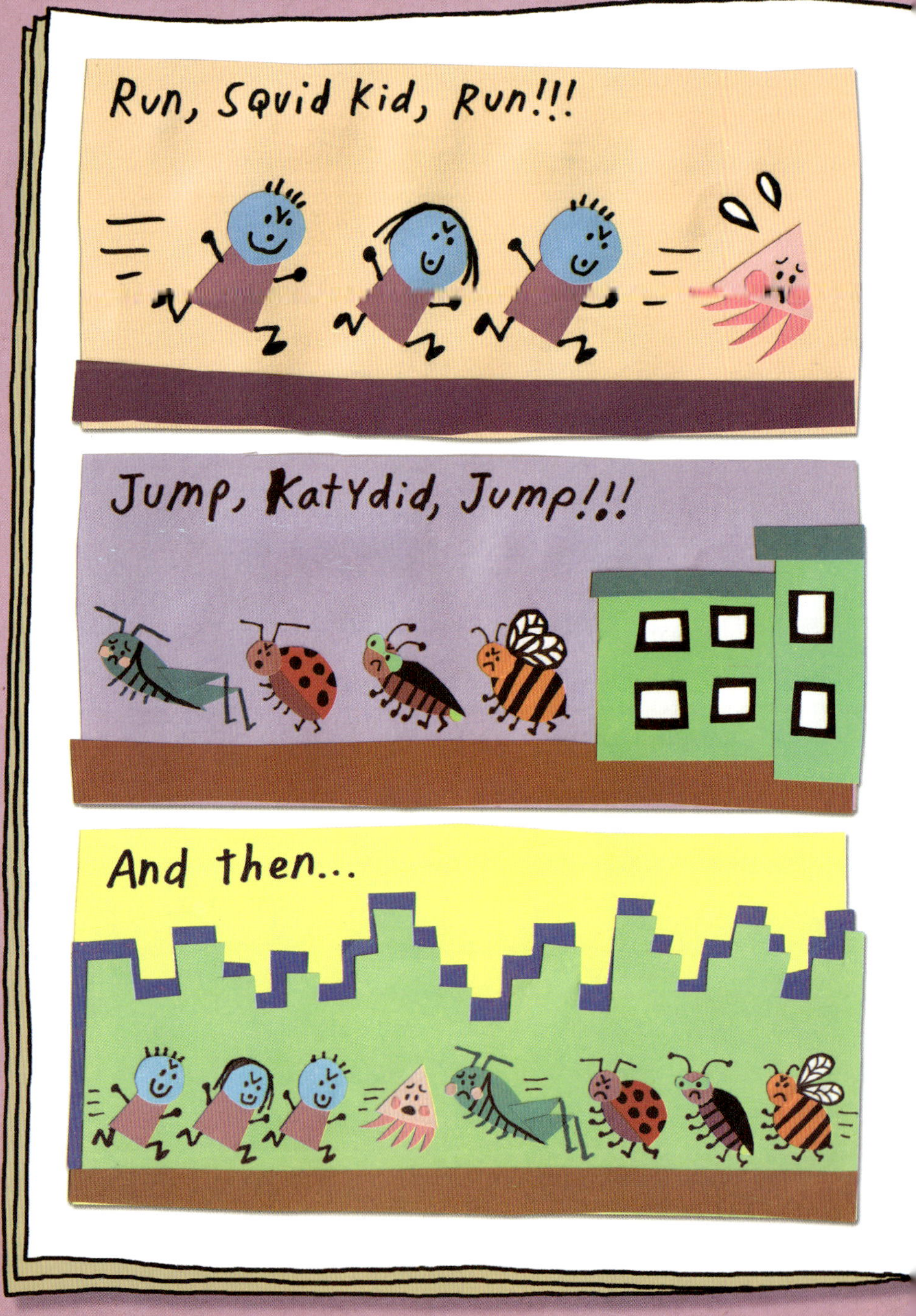

Jump, Katydid, Jump!!!

And then...

BONK!

... Just when everything seemed Hopeless...

SQUID Kid did Something extraordinary!
SSSSSSSSSSSSSSSS

SSSSSSSSSSSSSS

OH, NO!!! We're Purple People!!!
Thanks a LOT, SQUID KID!!!

SQUID Kid Felt embarrassed...

...BUT Katydid didn't.
HA! HA! HA! HA!

come on, SQUID KID!!!

Let's Go Change the World!!!!

Squid Kid felt nervous...
Down With Misfits

Down With Misfits
SSSSSSSS

...but Katydid didn't.
Boing

scribble
scribble

Boing!

Squid Kid felt unsure...
MisFits Go Home

SSSSSSSS
MisFits Go Home

... but Katydid didn't.
BoinG!

BoinG

SQuid Kid Felt Afraid...
CiTizens AGAinst MisFiTS

SSSSSSS
CiTizens AGAinst MisFiTS

...but katydid didn't.

Boing!

After a hard day of changing the WORLd...
Boing
Boing Boing

...They bounced to SQuid kid's house.
S.K.

SQuid Kid's Parents made pizza.

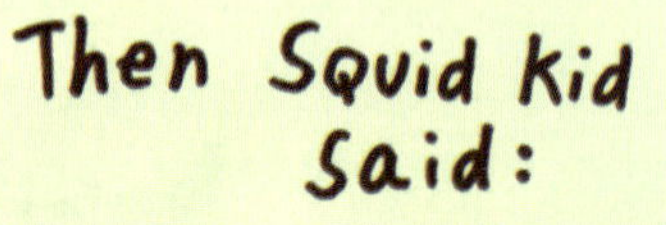
Then Squid Kid
Said:

Do You want to
be my BFF?

and Katydid...

...did.

The
END

Wow! That was really GOOD!!!
Thanks!

Did you like it, Daddy?

Yes, I did!

And do you feel better?

Actually, I **DO**!!!

Well then Get ready to RAISE the ROOF with JOY, Daddy...

...because it's time for...

BABY FROG SQUAD!

OH, YEAH! OH, YEAH!

WHOOP! WHOOP! BABY FROG SQUAD IN THE HOUSE!!!
BABY FROG

OH, YEAH! GIMME SOME! OH, YEAH!

BABY
FROG
SQUAD

Once upon a time...

... there were three baby frogs...

...Who went to the Police Academy.
COPS "Я" US

Frankie mastered Martial Arts...
CRACK

... C.C. mastered mechanical Arts...
CRANK
CRANK
CRANK
TOOLS

... and Boo mastered the art of witty RetorTS.
I Know You Are, but what am I?
HAW HAW

But soon they Got tired of working for the man.

I Know! Let's be Space heroes instead!
O.K.

...So Frankie, C.C. and Boo built a rocket ship...

...And they blasted off.
BOING

Space Door
Space Screen
Danger!
Soon, danger
was detected on Planet #39.

Oh, No!!! It's A BiG, Bad BULLY!!!

Let's Go!
Planet #39

So they landed...
FSSHHHHHH

KLONK

R-R-R-R-R

veeewp

ZOOOOOOM

Hey! We forgot our space suits!

I'm sure glad this planet has oxygen!
Me, too!

Soon our heroes met up with the bully.

HEY! CUT IT OUT!

Get Lost, worm breath!

I Know You are, but what am I?

HA HA
HA HA HA
HA HA
HA HA HA
That **Never** Gets old!

So You think You can Stop me with witty retorts, eh?

WELL Think AGAIN!

Say Hello to my little friend, Brutus!
SHOOoF

YAAAAAAAAAA!

Soon, Frankie, C.C., and Boo were CORNERED!

Bye-bye, Baby Frogs!

Why do you Gotta be so evil, Brutus?

It's Not my fault.

I was Programmed to be eviL!

NO WAY!

Yes way!

Ain't true!

IS, too!

Can't be!

Look and see!

meh.
Super evil
warm and cuddly

Hmmm...

meh.
Super evil.

meh.
and
cuddly

SLAM

Who wants a huG?

No Thanks.
I'll Pass.

I'll take one!

Do You Know who ELSE could use some Love???

whisper
whisper
whisper

That's a GREAT idea!

Tee-hee!

ZONG
IT'S SNUGGLE TIME!!!!

LET'S HUG it OUT!

YAAAAAAAAAA
Come BACK!!!

Our work is done!

HOORAY!!!

And so...

ZOOM

Our first mission was a SUPA SUCCESS!

Yeah... but I sure will miss that little pink robot.

ABOUT THE CREATORS:

Billie likes to make up stories and watch videos. She also likes sports and spiders.

El likes birds and dragonflies. They sing in a punk rock band with their brothers, Pink and Curly. It's called: "The Eye Screams."

Deb likes to make friendship bracelets and origami. She designed the characters in this comic.

Frida likes cereal.

Well? What did ya think, Daddy?

I thought it was **WONDERFUL!**

Thank You all for cheering me up!!!

Now Let's Go home and have a snack!
YAY!

This wasn't such a Sad Friday after all!
I Know! This chapter's title was **WAY OFF!**

Meanwhile...
HURRY up, Melvin!!!
I AM HURRY UPPinG!

Hey!!!

Where did everybody Go???

CHAPTER 9

NAOMI AND MELVIN REDEEM THEMSELVES (SORT OF)

A few minutes Later...
Hey! Where were you two?

We were working on our comics!

I finished my Punishment comic!

Do you want to see it?
Of course!!!

FEAST your EyeBALLS!!!

MY Sister, Naomi
A Graphic Poetry Jam
by Melvin the Frog

This is a jam about my Sister

and the Mister

who dismissed her.

Just a Fool at the Fair
who didn't Care.
Didn't see her There.
He didn't see the writer.
the Fighter.
the Fire Lighter.

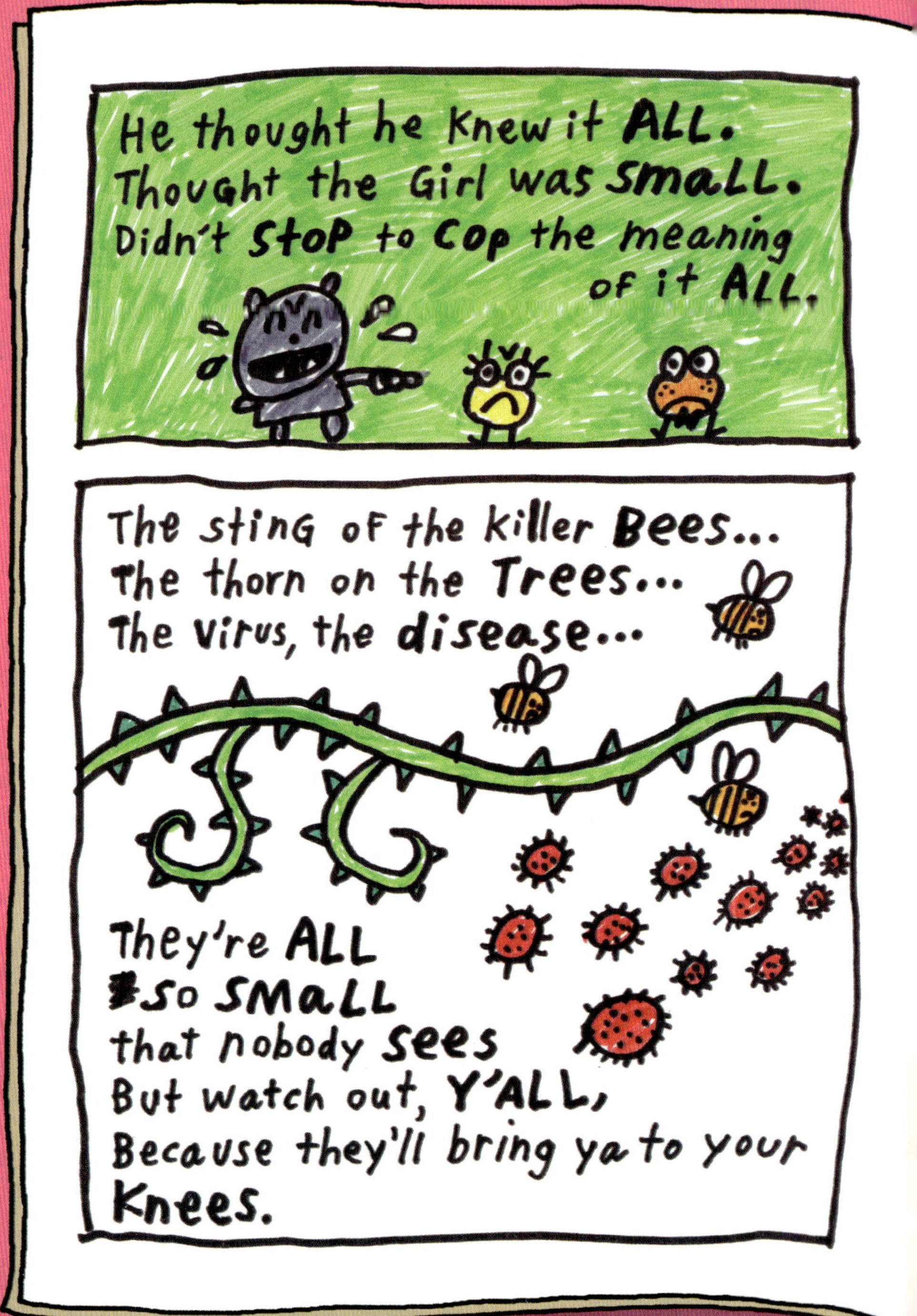

The sting of the killer Bees...
The thorn on the Trees...
The virus, the disease...

They're ALL
so SMALL
that nobody sees
But watch out, Y'ALL,
Because they'll bring ya to your
Knees.

Instead,
He shoulda stayed in Bed.
Shoulda listened what his momma said.

Shouldn'ta
Wouldn'ta
Landed on
his head.
POW

So Go on, be a **hater.**
Underestimate her.
But you better **Pray**
you **Stay**
outta her **WAY!**

As she tied
her web a little
tighter:

"I Guess I shoulda
Tried
to be a little
Brighter."

The END!!!

A Melvin's Media Megacorp Production

Written by: Melvin
Drawings by: Melvin
Edited by: Melvin
Costumes by: Melvin
Lettering by: Melvin

Art Production by: Melvin
Copyedited by: Melvin
backgrounds by: Melvin
Coloring by: Melvin
Publicity by: Melvin

Based on an original idea by: Melvin
Copyright by: Melvin. All rights reserved by: Melvin
Time-out rock sat on by: everybody EXCEPT Melvin

Well?

What did You think?

It was...

YOU TOUCHED MY HEART!!!
I touched MY heart, too!!!

You're MY FAVORITE Brother, Melvin!!!
HEY!

I THOUGHT I WAS YOUR FAVORITE!

Sorry, Kip. You Snooze, You Lose!

And Now it's MY TURN!!!

I'm not done Yet, So this is Just a PREVIEW!

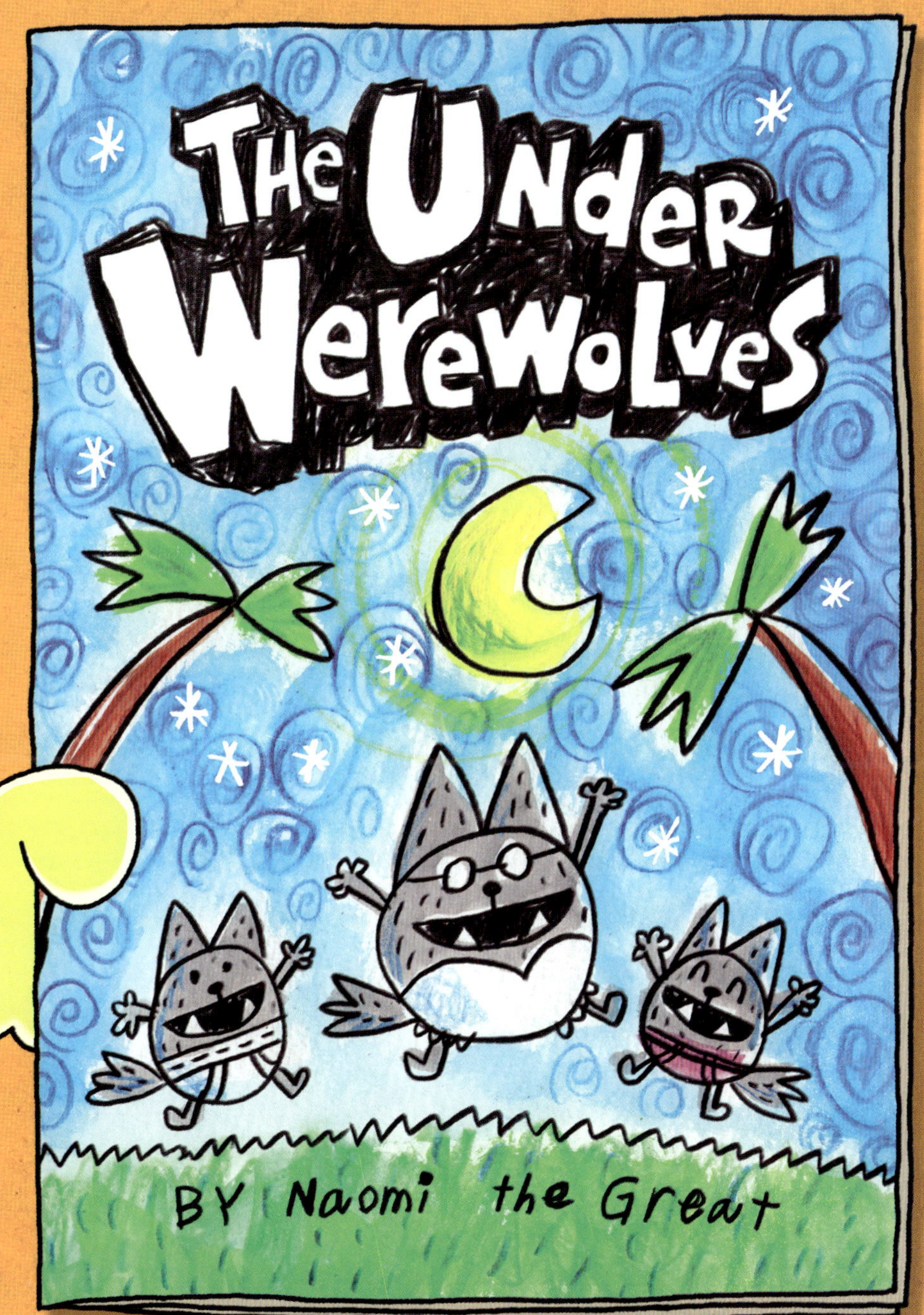
The Under Werewolves
BY Naomi the Great

Lou and Rose...

...would not wear clothes...

...but Grandma had a plan.

Underwear is fun to wear!!!

...and then the Joy Began.

But very soon, beneath the moon...

They came upon a sight!

For Down below a Fashion show...
Monster Fashion Show

...had turned into a Fight!!!
Monster Fashion Show

"I Am Dressed the Very Best!"
Each angry Monster said.

But Grandma knew just what to do...

... to change their minds instead.

WHat will she do...

(With Rose and Lou)

...to stop this crazy Game?

And teach the brawL:

Beneath it all...

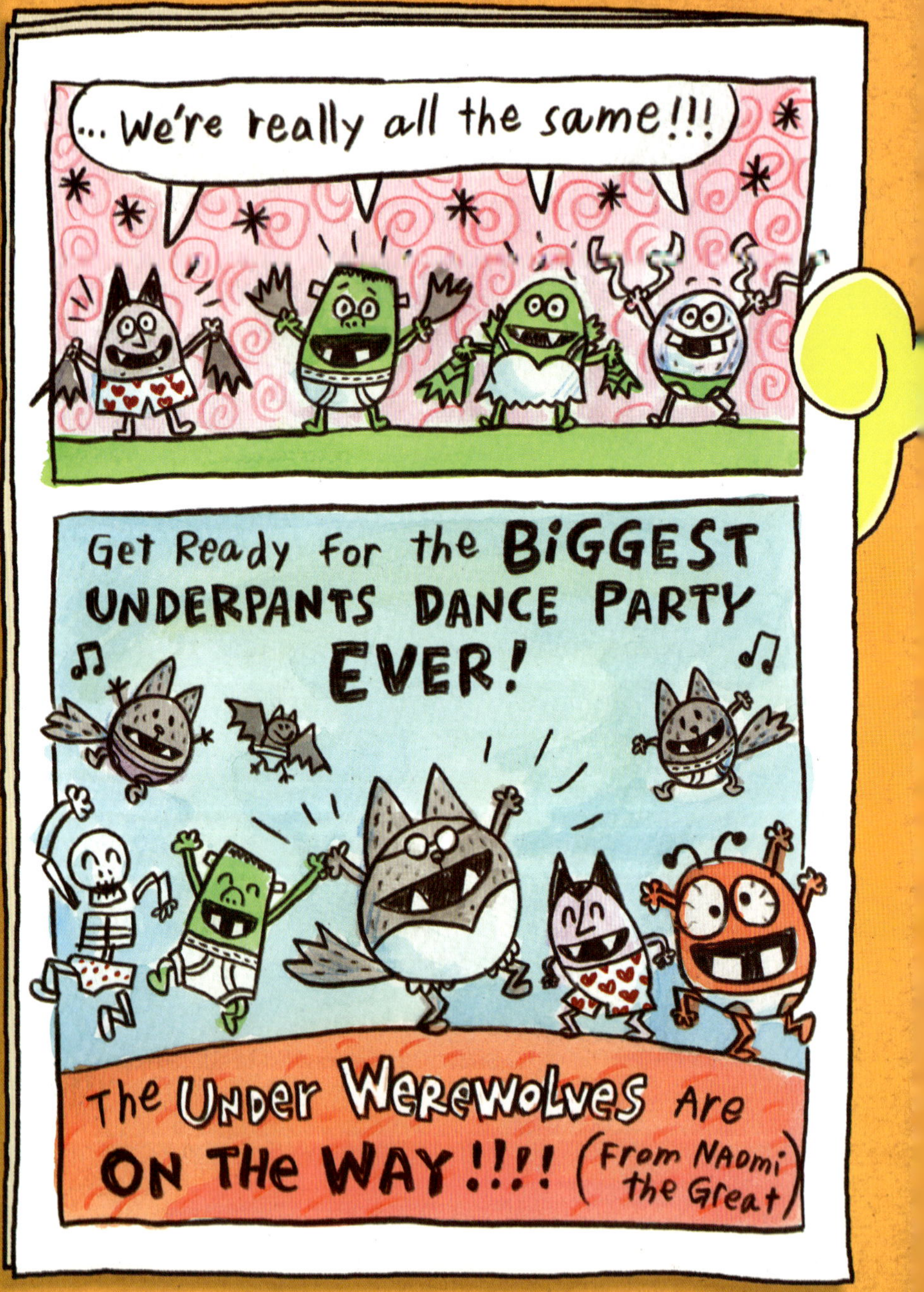

Get Ready for the BiGGEST UNDERPANTS DANCE PARTY EVER!

The UNDER WEREWOLVES Are ON THE WAY!!!! (From NAOMI the Great)

WOW! THAT WAS AWESOME!

NAOMI! We changed our minds!

Your comic preview was SO GOOD...

...that we want you to join the HACKER BROTHERS!

NOT SO FAST!

whisper whisper whisper

whisper whisper whisper

Okay!

So can we
WAiT!!!

One moment, please.

whisper whisper

snip

snip

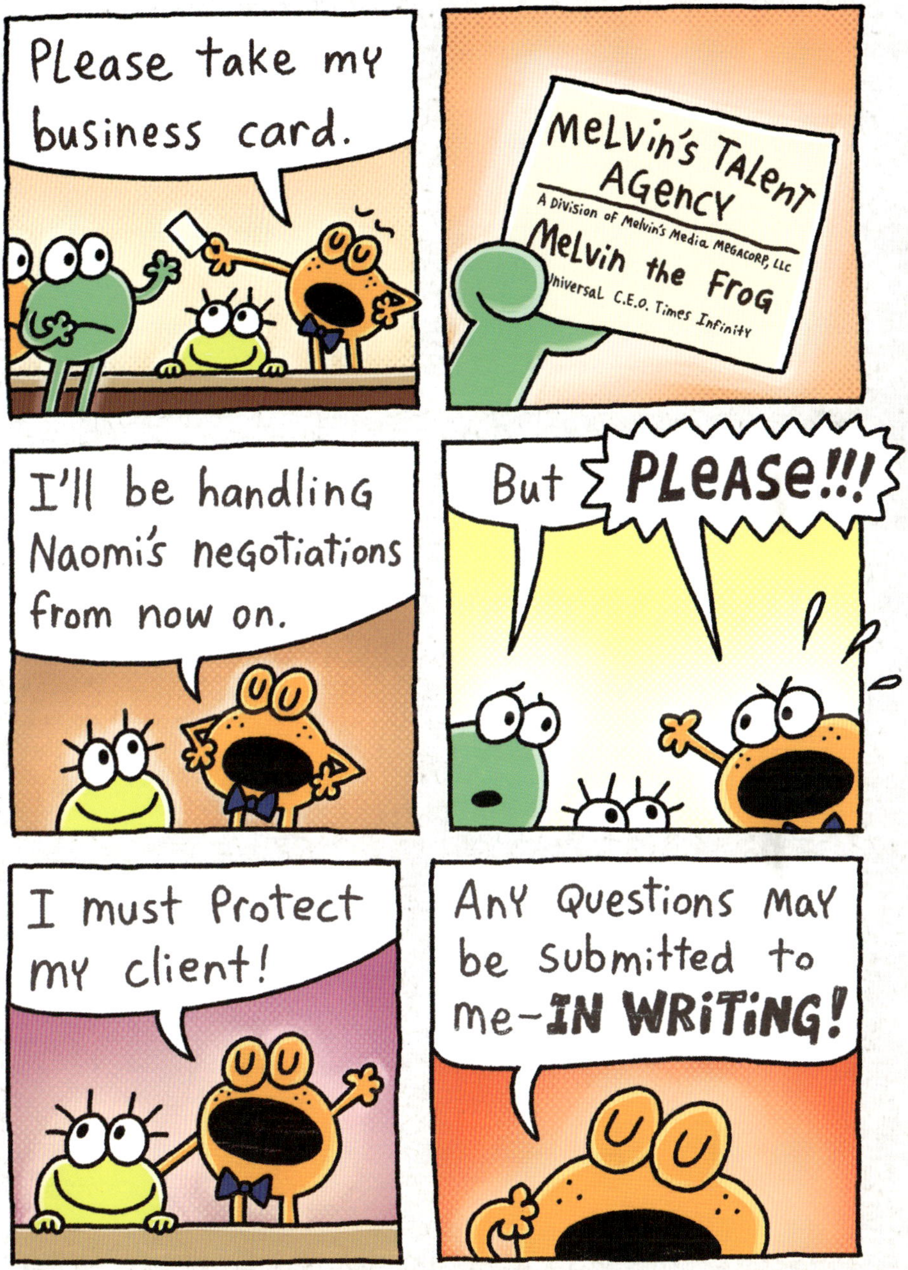

I'll be handling Naomi's negotiations from now on.

But
GOOD DAY, SIR!

Yeah, but
I SAID, GOOD DAY!

See, Daddy?

Melvin and Naomi are Best friends now!!!

And it's all because of YOU!

With your talent and my business savvy...

...We shall CRUSH All those who DARE to Stand Against us!

MWA HA-HA-HAW-HAW-HAW-HA

MWA HAW
HAW HAW
What HAVE I DONE?

CAN Melvin and Naomi Remain besties?

WILL FLIPPY Ever Stop worrying?

And WHO Are the Special Guest Stars Dashing forth to investigate???

FIND OUT IN OUR NEXT EPIC ADVENTURE!
CAT KID
COMIC CLUB
Book 3 COMING SOON!

NOTES & FUN FACTS

☆ Squids really **DO** spray ink when they feel threatened or scared. It's made of melanin, and it's usually blueish-black in color (not purple).

☆ Frankie, Boo, Brutus, and C.C. were all named after breakfast cereals.

☆ Naomi's dialogue on page 157 (panels 3 and 4) was based on a quote from Olivia Chaffin, a Girl Scout from Tennessee who boycotted the sale of Girl Scout cookies because they contain some palm oils that are linked to deforestation. Her online petition made international headlines.

☆ Chubbs and Jake's van is outfitted with an **ACTUAL WORKING DISCO** inside, including functioning stereo speakers, a mini subwoofer, 1970s faux-wood paneling, multicolored rotating disco lights, and a mirrored floor.

☆ The Baby Frog Squad's spaceship had to be rebuilt after the original one (from book #1) got sat on accidentally.

☆ The newly redesigned spaceship was made out of cardboard, duct tape, wire, hot glue, and magnets (which hold the legs up when in "Flying mode"). The eyes are plastic light bulb-shaped flashlights and they really light up!

☆ The little cars in BABY FROG SQUAD were made from the tops of Japanese salt containers (taped together) with rice-dough lips and toy "building block" wheels duct-taped underneath.

☆ On page 140, Summer really **IS** writing the Zen Shodo phrase, "Za Ichi So Shichi,"[1] which translates to "Sit First, dash Seven." It means: Start the day with meditation/prayer/mindfulness before dashing around.

---

1. Shozo Sato, *Shodo: The Quiet Art of Japanese Zen Calligraphy* (Rutland: Tuttle Publishing, 2014).

GET READING W

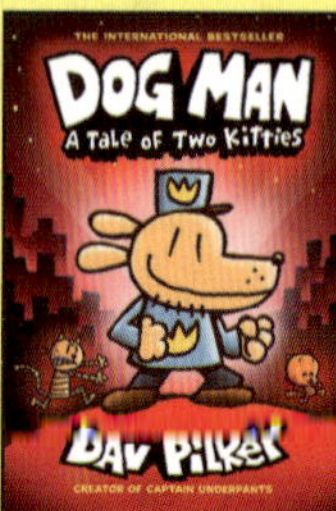

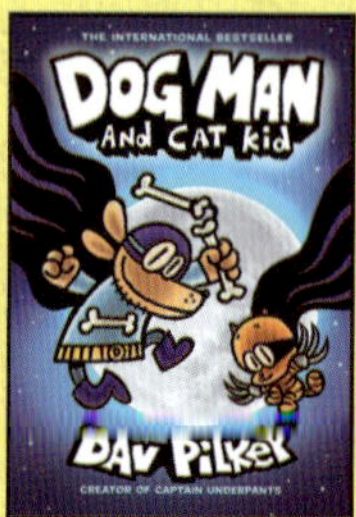

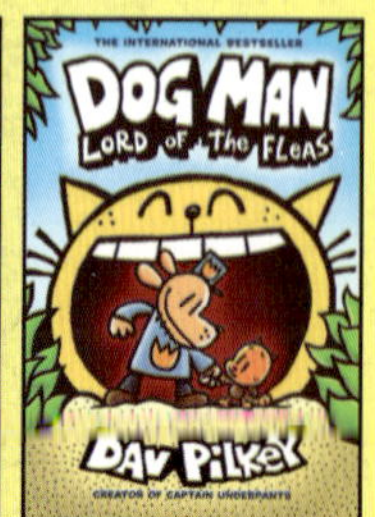

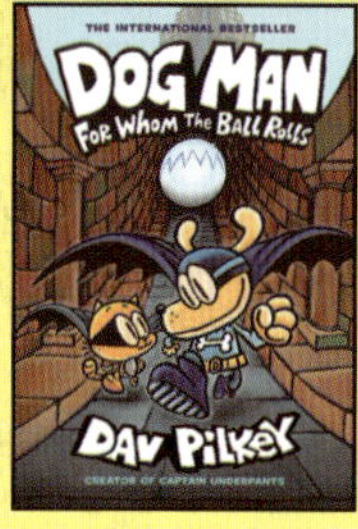

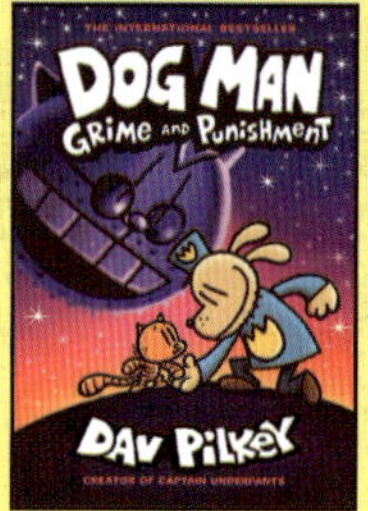

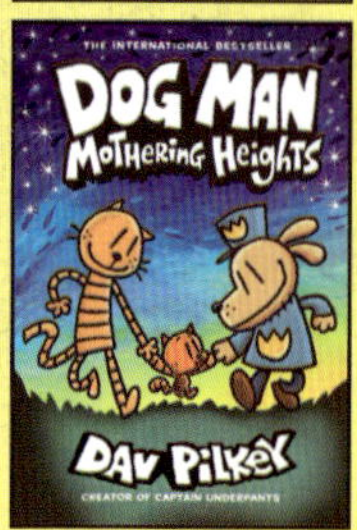

★ "Irreverent, laugh-out-loud funny, and . . . downright moving."
— Publishers Weekly, starred review

TH DAV PILKEY!

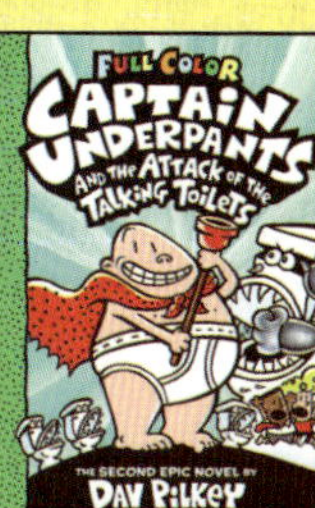
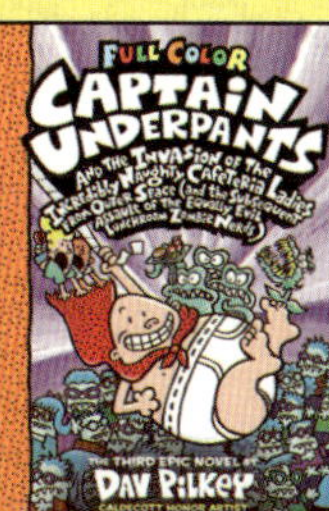
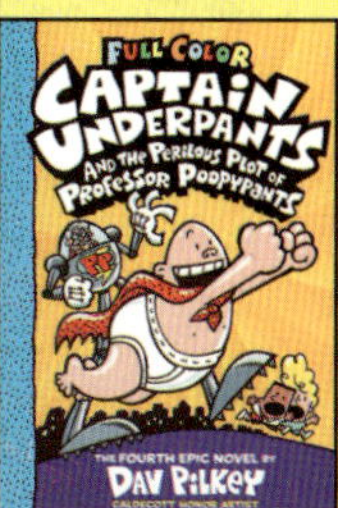
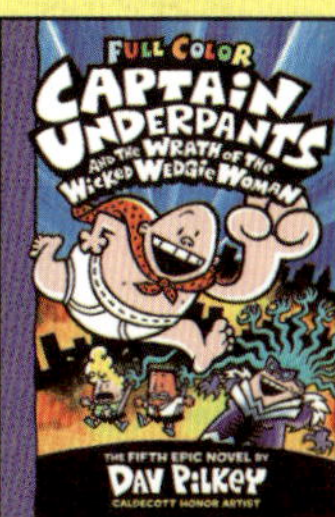

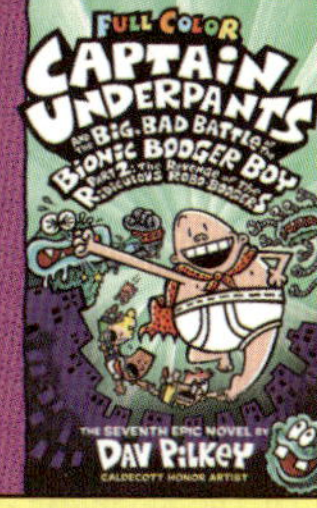
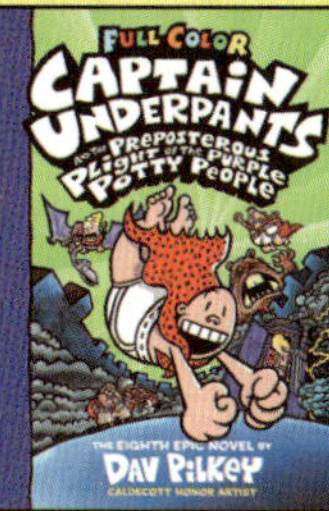
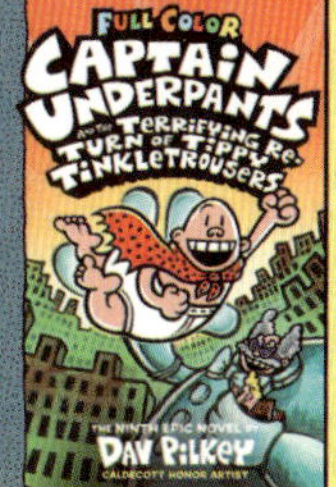

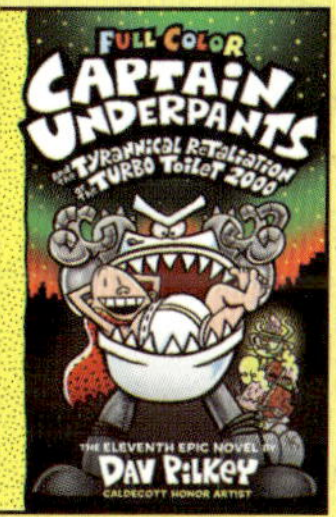

The epic musical adventure is now available from Broadway Records!

Go to planetpilkey.com to read chapters, make comics, watch videos, play games, and download supa fun stuff!

ABOUT THE AUTHOR-ILLUSTRATOR

When Dav Pilkey was a kid, he was diagnosed with ADHD and dyslexia. Dav was so disruptive in class that his teachers made him sit out in the hallway every day. Luckily, Dav loved to draw and make up stories. He spent his time in the hallway creating his own original comic books — the very first adventures of Dog Man and Captain Underpants.

In college, Dav met a teacher who encouraged him to write and illustrate for kids. He took her advice and created his first book, WORLD WAR WON, which won a national competition in 1986. Dav made many other books before being awarded the California Young Reader Medal for DOG BREATH (1994) and the Caldecott Honor for THE PAPERBOY (1996).

In 2002, Dav published his first full-length graphic novel for kids, called THE ADVENTURES OF SUPER DIAPER BABY. It was both a USA Today and New York Times bestseller. Since then, he has published more than a dozen full-length graphic novels for kids, including the bestselling Dog Man and Cat Kid Comic Club series.

Dav's stories are semi-autobiographical and explore universal themes that celebrate friendship, empathy, and the triumph of the good-hearted.

When he is not making books for kids, Dav loves to kayak with his wife in the Pacific Northwest.

Learn more at Pilkey.com.